Copyright © 2021 Nkechi Orabuchi-Fluker, AdaZion Educational Consulting, LLC.

All rights reserved. No part of this book may be produced or used in any manner without written permission of the copyright owner except for the use of quotations in a book review.

For more information or to request permissions, contact author at adazion.royalty@gmail.com.

The book is based on Genesis 2:15-3:24 KJV.

Paperback: ISBN 978-1-7364766-2-8

First paperback edition May 2021.

Written by Nkechi Orabuchi-Fluker
Illustrated by Ayan Mansoori

www.adazioneducationalconsulting.com

I0099206

"Hi Mom! What are you doing?" Chibu asked with joy.

His mom responded, "Making some smoothies for breakfast. How are you doing? You look like you have something on your mind."

Chibu responded, "I was wondering if I could go to the Bounce House event with my friends from online school?"

"What did your dad say?" His mom asked. Chibu slowly responded that his dad had said no. He perked up, "But it does not really mean no if you say yes!"

His mother turned to him and firmly stated, "Your dad said no and obedience to this matter is important. You asking this way reminds me of a story. Remember when your dad talked to you about the creation? Well, The Most High Yah created man on the sixth day from the dust of the ground. The Most High's very own breath brought him to life and He put him in the garden of Eden."

"The garden was so beautiful! You could see His creation all together in harmony. The Most High gave the man the responsibility of taking care of the garden. In the midst of the garden was the tree of life and the tree of the knowledge of good and evil. The instruction was given directly to man that he could eat from any tree except from the tree of the knowledge of good and evil. If he ate from that tree, he would die."

"Adam named all the animals. Now, The Most High Yah said, 'It is not good for man to be alone. I will make him a help meet for him'. He then created a suitable helper for Adam. The Most High put Adam to a deep sleep and took one of his ribs to make the woman. Adam called her woman because she came from him. Therefore, a man will leave his father and mother and be joined together with his wife to become one flesh. Although they were naked in the garden as man and wife, they were not ashamed."

"In the garden one of the animals, the serpent, slyly said to the woman, 'Did The Most High say that you should not eat of every tree of the garden?' The woman replied that they could eat from any tree in the garden except from the tree of the knowledge of good and evil. They also could not touch it or they would die. The serpent told the woman that they would not die, but rather they would be like gods knowing good and evil. Because of what the serpent said, she saw the tree to be good for food, it was pleasing to her eyes, and she thought it would make her wise. She ate from it and also gave it to her husband to eat with her."

"Their eyes were opened and they realized they were naked! So they sewed fig leaves to cover themselves. As they heard the voice of The Most High Yah walking in the garden, they hid from Him amongst the trees. The Most High Yah called unto Adam to ask him where he had hidden. Adam answered that he heard The Most High's voice and was afraid because he was naked."

"The Most High Yah asked them, 'Who told you that you were naked? Did you eat from the tree that I commanded you not to eat from?' The man answered that it was the woman who was given to him who caused him to eat from the tree. The Most High asked the woman what she did and she said she was deceived by the serpent to eat from the tree."

"The serpent's act led The Most High to curse him above all animals. He ended up on his belly to eat dust all the days of his life. The Most High also put a hatred between the serpent and the woman and between their seeds. He greatly multiplied the woman's sorrow and birth pains so she would have pain when having children. Also, that she would have a desire for her husband, but he would rule over her. Then He said to Adam because he listened to his wife in this situation and ate from the tree that he was directly commanded not to do, the ground would be cursed because of him and in sorrow he would eat of it all the days of his life. Also, in pain he would eat from it by the sweat of his face. From dust he came and to dust he will return."

"Adam called his wife Eve because she is the mother of all living. The Most High Yah made coats of skin to cover them. And The Most High Yah said, 'Behold, the man has become like one of us, to know good and evil. He may try to also take food from the tree of life, eat, and live forever.' The Most High sent him out of the garden of Eden to till the ground where he was created from. He placed Cherubims and a flaming sword to fully guard the tree of life."

"Wow! That is sad. Disobedience leads to consequences." Chibu stated.

His mom exclaimed, "That is right! I just want you to be clear that since your dad said no, I am in agreement with it because we are one working together for your good. Also, we never want to twist anyone's words or be sneaky about a situation. It is better to be honest, obey righteous instructions, and be at peace."

Chibu replied, "I get it. I definitely do not want to twist anyone's words. If Adam and his wife had listened to The Most High, then they would have been able to still enjoy the garden."

"That is true. And their fall has affected us until this day. Thankfully, we have the opportunity to repent of our sins and be forgiven through the Messiah. As long as we have the faith of Messiah and keep The Most High's commandments, we can be restored back to Him."

Chibu hugged his mom and thanked her.

THE FALL OF MANKIND LEARNING ACTIVITY

1. Eve was created from which part of Adam's body?
   a. Feet
   b. Head
   c. Rib
   d. Hand

2. What tree were Adam and Eve commanded not to eat from?
   a. The Tree of Life
   b. The Pear Tree
   c. The Apple Tree
   d. The Tree of Knowledge of Good and Evil

3. What animal tempted Eve to break the commandment of The Most High Yah?
   a. Lion
   b. Serpent
   c. Bear
   d. Tiger

4. What fruit did Eve eat from the tree?
   a. Apple
   b. Pear
   c. It does not say
   d. Berries

5. List out the consequences of breaking The Most High's commandment for each creation:
   a. Adam-
   b. Eve-
   c. serpent-

In your own words, what was the lesson that Chibu learned?

www.ingramcontent.com/pod-product-compliance
Lightning Source LLC
Chambersburg PA
CBHW041558040426

42447CB00002B/219